LOOK
AWAY
FROM
DIXIE

LOOK
AWAY
FROM
DIXIE

《 》

FRANK E. SMITH

louisiana state university press

PREFACE

Since my involuntary retirement from the House of Representatives in 1962, I have been attempting to meet a responsibility for comment upon public issues especially relevant to my political experience. The theme of my expression has been that the century-old influence of racist politics has so gripped all Southern institutions that the whole nation has suffered, not only the South. Great opportunity now exists for the South to turn away from its ancient, unhealthy preoccupation, and the national interest demands it.

My book, *Congressman from Mississippi,* has been my

chief effort to present the details of the cancerous influence of racism on Southern political life, but I have elaborated upon this theme in talks and magazine articles. An understanding of the full effect of racist politics is essential if the South is to take advantage of the present opportunity to fully enter the mainstream of American life.

The articles grouped together in this volume are the result of an effort to explain this viewpoint. One of them, "The Changing South," was first published in 1955, but it was even then an attempt to express the same general thought. I have considered it worth including in this volume, in addition to the others, because it is an example of the inhibitions of expression placed upon a Southern politician. The article was written a few months after the 1954 school desegregation decision by the Supreme Court, but I had virtually to ignore the decision and its impact upon the South because it would have been politically impossible for me to discuss it with truth and realism.

The futile decade of Southern resistance to integration made very unrealistic my prediction of the South's joining the mainstream of American life. The Negro revolution is in process, however, and it removes the last barrier to full-scale Southern entry into the national life, as I suggest in "The Emerging South." Both of these articles were originally published in the *Virginia Quarterly Review*, the first in the thirtieth anniversary edition of that magazine in 1955, and the second in the fortieth anniversary edition in 1965. Permission to reprint these two essays has been granted by the editors; and the *South Atlantic Quarterly* has permitted the reprinting of "Valor's Second Prize." "The Pattern of Southern Congressional Politics" is a revision of an article originally published in *The Nation,* for which permission to reprint has also been granted.

I want to express my appreciation for the assistance of my secretary, Mrs. Mary Knurr, in the preparation of the manuscript, and for the invaluable help of my former assistant, Mrs. Audrey Warren.

FRANK E. SMITH

KNOXVILLE, TENNESSEE
FEBRUARY, 1965

CONTENTS

ix

LOOK
AWAY
FROM
DIXIE

Look Away from Dixie

THE SOUTH . . . THE POOR SOUTH . . ." JOHN C. Calhoun died with this lament upon his lips. Henry W. Grady, a Southern patriot of less national significance, died with a similar plaintive cry. In between these two great Southerners, who met natural deaths, were many thousands of others who died of battle wounds, hunger, and disease, with the same regret for their beloved South. The South as a symbol has absorbed so much of the energy and ability of white Southerners through the past century that it is worth considering whether the very concept of the term has any future value for the nation, or even for those who live in the South.

3

A popular theory in the South is that the romanticized "Gone With the Wind" concept of the fabled antebellum South was a defense mechanism developed by the defeated generation after the Civil War to justify its bitter and costly resistance and the postwar years of poverty. Whatever the merits of this theory, Southern introversion after the Civil War certainly developed the most sharply defined regional inferiority complex to be found anywhere in the United States. One tragic result of the complex has been the South's unwillingness to enter fully many national arenas, but its most objectionable outgrowth has been a chip on the entire regional shoulder, with a resultant tendency to blame every deficiency on a massive "Northern" or "outside" effort to take advantage of a people irreparably weakened by war and Reconstruction. The Southern mind has excused regional deficiencies, both to itself and to outsiders, by the usually accurate, if irrelevant, defense that there was always a worse condition somewhere up North.

Like the insecure individual who sees a slight in every casual encounter and concludes that the world is against him, the South has conjured up the spectre of a "conspiracy" against it by the rest of the country. Acceptance of the conspiracy theory was so all pervasive that as late as 1942 the scholarly president of the Southern Historical Association repeated Calhoun's words, ". . . the poor South," and blamed the ills of the region on both the Republicans and the Democrats, on federal relief—and on the inequitable distribution of federal relief—on absentee ownership of newspapers and industries, on New Deal Democrats who envisioned increased industrialization, on lower Works Progress Administration (WPA) wage rates in the South, and on the union requirements that Southern miners be paid the same scale as miners in the North. The real crux of this complaint was revealed, however, in the statement that ". . . the South [was] not free to integrate itself" and that "disenfranchisement of the Negro, occasional race riots, and the sporadic mobbing of Negroes" were unfairly criticized in the North which "either could not or would not understand the necessity of race segregation."

So deeply imbedded are the many aspects of this elaborate defense mechanism that, in spite of the major progress in eliminating the economic ills from which the whole fiction was spawned, they have carried over undiminished into the racial strife of the past ten years. Thus the white South has continued to tell itself—and attempted to tell the rest of the country—that Southern Negroes are a happy, docile, carefree people until subversive outsiders stir them up for political purposes; and otherwise intelligent people have accepted the assertion that the murder of civil-rights workers was nothing more than a hoax. Its unremitting repetition over the passing years has transformed the once plaintive defense into a strident philosophy that tolerates no dissenting voice. Any Southerner who points to deficiencies in Southern life is a scalawag in the worst tradition of the Reconstruction period, which automatically proves that anything he says is a nefarious lie.

One of the small, but significant, disadvantages of the complete insistence upon southernness in the South has been the tendency to use only things Southern as a basis for comparison. This may not matter very much if it is only a hotel, or department store, or restaurant that is "one of the best in the South," or "as good as any in the South." But standards deteriorate when important comparisons are confined within regional limits; and the deterioration when schools, colleges, churches, and local government have been meaningfully compared only within these Southern limits has been extremely harmful to all of the South.

The very term "Southerner"—as used here and just about everywhere else—is a misnomer unless qualified with the word "white." It is habitually used to describe attitudes and beliefs obviously not shared by the 25 percent or so of the Southern population that is Negro.

All of the Confederate states went through some period of a near-solidified white effort to overturn Reconstruction rule and to secure white domination of the political, economic, and social order. The effort required subservience of every aspect of life to racial distinctions, and it produced a South linked together by race. This has been the only real base for Southern unity in the current generation. If we are now ending the racial South, is it worthwhile trying to keep any other?

Actually there have been many Souths, crisscrossing state boundaries and definable on the bases of economic, racial, and topographic lines. The lower Mississippi Valley is the center of an alluvial plain covering parts of six states but with remarkable homogeneity. The comparable Tennessee Valley touches parts of seven states, but at least three distinct regions are included in the overall watershed. The different Souths have never been the same except on issues directly related to race.

It is popular to attribute race attitudes in different parts of the South to factors like economic patterns and ratios between white and Negro population. This has been true in broad generality, as demonstrated by the fact that the highest percentage of Negro population is included in the Deep South states which have been strongest in their support of segregation. There are many obvious exceptions to the rule, however, which greatly weaken its validity: for example, the sharply differing reactions to racial change between otherwise almost identical counties lying side by side, with only the Tennessee-Mississippi boundary between them; and the fact that the first town in Mississippi to agree to a school-desegregation program without the threat of a court order was Greenville, in the heart of the state's Delta region, with approximately a 50–50 Negro-white population proportion. The differing traditions of state political leadership and the qualities of personal leadership are the best answers to the puzzles that seem to surface here.

From the days of Reconstruction onward, the South has passed through a succession of "New Souths." In most cases the phrase has been a slogan to promote an idea that represented economic, cultural, or social progress in the South. Henry W. Grady first brought the phrase into general use with his campaign for industrialization and friendly acceptance of Northern capital. Since that time almost every campaign for economic improvement has had elements of the Grady "New South" concept.

Throughout this century the "New South" has been the theme of campaigns and movements to eliminate provincial cultural dogmas and establish standards more in keeping with those of the country as a whole. For many today the words mean rising commercial and industrial development, accompanying urbanization, and the general change in the pace and pattern of living.

In the 1930's, "New South" largely referred to the economic reforms and improvement designed primarily for the Southern states as part of the New Deal's overall effort. In the years since World War II, the term has come to be accepted as including the goal of eliminating racial injustice and discrimination. It has been used by the activists in the effort (*New South* is the name of the publication of the Southern Regional Council), and it has been used also by those who have not necessarily pushed, but have been willing to accept, the changing racial order.

Whatever their limitations of purpose or failures of achievement, the New South campaigns have all been on the side of improving Southern life. Basically they have all been an attempt to bring Southern life closer to a full participation in the national life. They have all grown from the conviction that a "New South" would give Southerners a better share of the fruits of America—economically, culturally, socially, politically. Today the concept seems outmoded. Why not plan and act on the principle that what is needed is not a New South but a South that is inextricably and indefinably a part of the entire United States? The several "Old Souths" can be studied and analyzed for years as part of the history of our country, but what purpose is there in the future South's being anything but a geographic definition of a large and populous part of the United States?

A generation ago, when the geographic South was a national economic problem, many aspects of that problem could properly and beneficially be attacked on a basis of their regional characteristics—outmoded agricultural practices, absentee industrial ownership and management, restrictive freight rates, poor health and poor education. The New Deal reforms of that day, supplemented by the economic stimulus of World War II and the postwar prosperity, have eliminated most of the acute regional economic problems. Economic problems remain, it is true, but they are facets of national problems—the effect of unequal and discriminatory education and the near permanent burdens of specific agricultural commodities, to name two immediate ones. Very few economic problems in the South today

are susceptible to regional solutions, and very little attempt is being made to achieve any.

The South today is in the midst of many problems, and
many of them arise from that which is distinctly
Southern—the heritage of Negro slavery and the century of
denial of the Negro rights that were supposedly guaranteed
by the constitutional changes following the Civil War.
Racial problems in the United States have never been
confined to the South, and they certainly are not confined
to the current South. There are some distinctly Southern
aspects of these problems, however, and they cannot be
swept under or away by merely calling attention to the
various racial transgressions and conflicts which are peculiar to other regions or common to the whole country.

Race is the only problem still common to the historic
South—those states that were part of the Confederacy.
These states have used both law and custom to maintain
the separate but equal doctrine and have regarded as one
of the primary state prerogatives the right to perpetuate
segregation and discrimination by law, even in violation of
the Constitution. Today the border and upper South states
have responded to Negro demands and to national public
opinion and national law, and a relatively rapid process of
dismantling official barriers to integration is under way.
The upper South, the last area to embrace the myth of a
successful Confederacy, was naturally the first area to over-
come the similar myth of successful massive resistance to
integration and other aspects of the Negro revolution. The

lower South has not yet fully discarded the myth, in spite of widespread recognition of its inevitable collapse.

Pressures from without the South, in the form of public opinion, economic realities, and federal law, are making certain the racial change in the South, but the final decision as to how it will be accepted is still to be made in the South. These are perhaps the final decisions that the South should make as a distinct, separate part of the nation. Perhaps it would be romantically fitting for the South to make this decision as a region, a geographic region which has been made a political and social entity almost entirely on the strength of a racial philosophy, but it is not very likely to happen that way. The South in reality is not a regional entity; thus the decision is being made according to the economic and philosophic dictates of individual areas within the geographic region.

The extent of change was reflected in the vote in the 1964 presidential election, but it has been demonstrated most clearly in the acceptance of school desegregation and the general relaxation of other racial barriers in the years 1961–64. No part of the South is a pattern of perfect racial harmony, but those areas which first saw the futility of the massive-resistance doctrine have reaped the benefit of relative absence of tension and violence. The communities operating biracial committees, either formal or informal, have almost all felt their immediate advantage. There is a longer range advantage which is equally obvious—the racial revolution in these communities has been achieved

with only a few serious wounds, and the healing scars are
going to be far easier to overlook in the generations
ahead.

The Civil Rights Act of 1964 has been more than a
Magna Carta for Negro citizens; it has freed the Southern
white moderate from the oppressive restrictions which
have so effectively silenced him heretofore. There no
longer need be agonizing decisions as to whether a community project will be available to Negroes, how Negroes will
be served by a business, or whether they can be ignored as
part of the labor force. In most of the South there is no
longer a choice as to whether they can be ignored as a
political force. The politician who does will do so at his
own peril, in terms of both Negro support and opposition
and the growing evidence that the majority of the white
electorate will no longer tolerate racial demagoguery.

The time has come for the South's leaders in every field
to recognize that the elimination of racial barriers is more
than just the easing of the tensions and troubles of today.
Solutions must be achieved that point the way toward full
participation by Negro citizens in community life, if that
life is to realize the full American potential. Negroes are
going to remain a major part of the South's population for
the foreseeable future. A significant amount of our national governmental effort is being dedicated to ensuring
that they do not remain second-class citizens. Where they
are willingly given an opportunity to share in community

growth and development through their own efforts, they are naturally going to make the greatest contribution.

The necessity for full participation by Negro leaders in charting the future course for Southern states, cities, and communities is another very evident reason why the South must turn away from the Dixieland concept of itself. Entirely too much of that concept is more than Negro Americans can accept as the precept and mores of their home communities and states, because the concept is not merely a heritage of the Confederacy, it is the long tradition of building all institutions and all society around the fundamental theme, spoken or unspoken, of white supremacy. The free Negro citizen cannot live with that.

We cannot rewrite history, but we can meet with strength the urgent requirement to build a new concept of society, in order that all may share its potential reward. The history will remain, to reveal, unravel, and interpret. There is a difference between changing the words of Stephen Foster's songs and merely refraining from playing "Old Black Joe" in the biracial schools of the future. The "Gone With the Wind," "Uncle Tom" version of the pre-Civil War South is just as inaccurate as "The Birth of a Nation" version of Reconstruction. The real history of the region has warts and pimples for both races, but the Dixieland tradition obscures the blemishes for the whites and omits or degrades the role of the Negro.

Eliminating the Confederate preoccupation from the

views of coming Southern generations will not diminish appreciation of the contribution the Southern states and their leaders have made to the best that is American. Virginia's contribution to the new Republic was Virginian, not Southern, though it was in good part made possible by the life of the Virginia plantation which provided that relative luxury for the wealthier class which encouraged all men of intellect and ability to develop those qualities. It is easy to describe Washington, Jefferson, Madison, and Mason as Virginians as well as Americans, but there is little about their careers that fits the traditional Southern label. Robert E. Lee has been the most revered Southern hero, but there can be little doubt that his decision to join the Confederate Army was determined by loyalty to Virginia rather than to the South. Lee accepted the war's decision as the federal supremacy over the states. The use that his name and the Confederate flag have been put to in the past decade, in defending or proudly proclaiming hate and bigotry and worse, has made it far more difficult for future historians to separate fact from legend in establishing a true picture of the impact of the Confederacy and its leaders on the country.

The whole story of the South for a century has been that of an effort to recapture the past while reaping the benefits of the constant change that has been America. More and more Southerners have rebelled at the burden of conscience involved in defending the segregated society with its pattern of racial injustice, and now they have been joined by many more who rebel at the sheer waste of time and energy in attempting to defeat the Negro revolution now supported by both law and national opinion.

Whatever the motivation of the individual Southerner, it is the result of national rather than Southern influence—the American ideal of liberty and justice and the American concept of majority rule by law. If these influences are bringing about the final decisive overthrow of the racist attitude that has dominated all institutions of the geographic South for so long, then there will no longer be anything but a geographic South. All but purely geographic groups or institutions have been Southern only because they shared an interest in defending, actively or passively, the peculiar Southern institution of segregation.

The Southern states are in the process of turning their backs upon racial discrimination and injustice, primarily because realization has at last come both to the nation and to a large part of the Southern population, both white and black, that the condition is wrong and there is no longer any need to put up with it. The positive side of the coin has not yet been examined.

The great advantage of the new order will be that it will be made stronger and richer by the contribution of well-educated and self-reliant Negro citizens, proudly conscious of the fact that they have achieved the promise of American life for all citizens. The Old South offered them little, and it is no excuse that the rest of the nation condoned this inequality. To be truly American citizens has been their hope, and it should also have been the hope of all the white South. If they realize that hope together, as they must, the South will have to look away from Dixie and forward to America.

Valor's Second Prize

THE TRADITION OF SOUTHERN INTERNATIONALISM HAS seemed, for the last twenty years, more legend than reality. In the mire of isolationist sentiment that seems to grip the South today, it is easy to forget that before World War II a considerable part of the strength behind our international policies had deep roots in the South. Part of its antecedent philosophy was the expansionist doctrine of slaveholders seeking new territory and the interventionist chauvinism of frontier nationalists. The economic motivation was an agricultural economy dependent upon export sales of cotton and tobacco, but this was little different from the motivations of the metropolitan port cities of the East.

The personal dedication of Cordell Hull to the ideal of low tariffs achieved through reciprocal trade agreements was reflected in the attitudes of many other Southern congressmen of the same period. Without it the reciprocal trade concept could not have been so firmly implanted in the congressional mind as to resist the heavy attacks it has withstood during the past decade. In the fifty years prior to the New Deal, the areas of universal agreement in the Democratic party of the North and the South were low tariffs and a liberal foreign trade policy, even though distinct differences had begun to develop in some of the sheep and mineral areas of the West.

The strongest support for Woodrow Wilson's League of Nations came from Southern senators. One of them, John Sharp Williams of Mississippi, refused to seek another term in his disgust with the mood of his colleagues, saying: "I'd rather be a hound dog and bay the moon" than remain in that body. Williams' Mississippi colleague, James K. Vardaman, had been one of the "little group of willful men" who fought any type of intervention in World War I. Vardaman, along with several other Southerners, makes it clear that there was a streak of Southern isolationism even at that date, but Vardaman's career also demonstrates the general state of public sentiment. Although "the great white chief" was considered one of the master orators and political demagogues of his day in Mississippi politics, he was easily defeated in 1918 by Congressman Pat Harrison, as one result of the reaction to his antiwar record of the previous year.

Among Southern members of Congress the years of World War II brought the same expressions of internationalist conviction that had existed in the League of Nations days. Southerners were the chief source of Democratic leadership for the legislation which the period called for. By the same token, there was also some isolationist sentiment among the Southern members, probably in about the same general proportion as had existed in 1917.

The first great test of internationalism in the post-World War II period was the authorization of the Marshall Plan. It passed with overwhelming Southern support in both Houses, but not before an intensive campaign by the cotton and tobacco industries to show the economic advantages of the plan to the South. Two Southerners, Tom Connally of Texas and Walter George of Georgia, were recent chairmen of the Senate Foreign Relations Committee. Both were generally cautious in their internationalism, but in their old age both saw fit to retire voluntarily from the Senate rather than face campaigns for renomination that would have been bitterly fought, with "internationalism" and "foreign aid" as the major issues.

Since the enactment of the Marshall Plan in 1948, the annual authorization and appropriation for foreign aid have become the major tests of internationalism in the

Congress. There still are many defects in the overall foreign aid program (and there have been many more) , but
the annual continuation of the program has through the
years been the real test of the internationalist feelings of
the members. In the years since 1960 a few sincere members have raised serious doubts about the value of various
phases of the program and the emphasis upon military
support where there were questions of its need. Occasionally, some of these have voted against one of the annual
bills as a means of registering a protest. These occasions
have been rare, however. Most of those who have voted
against a foreign aid bill and then labeled their vote as a
"protest" have simply been yielding to the personal luxury
of voting against a politically unpopular program. The
voting records through the years make this very clear.

Using the votes on foreign aid as a measuring device,
Southern members of Congress have steadily moved away
from internationalist concepts. From a peak of well over
three quarters of the members in both Houses to a bottom
of from one quarter to one third of the House and Senate,
the Southern votes in favor of the aid programs have
sharply declined. On international issues other than the
specific aid program the change has sometimes been even
more spectacular, and invariably as certain. The old free-
trade South has become a center of opposition to the reciprocal trade program.

In the fights over the neutrality issue prior to World War
II, and even in the postwar years, the Midwest came to be

identified as the center of isolationism. In recent years, however, there has been slightly stronger support for the United Nations from Midwestern congressmen than from the Southern members, and on most other international issues the percentage of yea and nay votes from those two areas has been largely the same. One reason for this is the growth of the Democratic party in the Midwest, but the change also reflects a change in public sentiment.

The traditional terms "isolationist" and "internationalist" are not precisely suitable to define the position of members of Congress on international issues. It is not likely that any member of Congress would willingly accept the label "isolationist," and some of those who most violently reject almost any form of international cooperation are strongest in their demands for extreme American intervention in many overseas areas. By the same token, although many Southern congressmen are obviously internationalist in their viewpoints, the label "internationalist" has become politically impossible for them.

One of the recent students in this field, Charles O. Lerche, Jr., is the author of a stimulating study of Southern congressmen's attitudes on foreign policy entitled "The Uncertain South." Unfortunately, the book misses the basic motivation of the great majority of the Southern congressmen who maintained an internationalist position. It also overlooks some obvious explanations of changes in voting patterns.

For example, Lerche makes something of a mystery of

the switch to total opposition to foreign aid in South Carolina in the middle of the decade, overlooking the fact that
it came after the retirement of Representative James C.
Richards, chairman of the Foreign Affairs Committee and
the man who handled the foreign aid authorizations on the
floor. He also fails to connect a major switch against aid in
Georgia, which followed the retirement of Senator Walter
George. No analysis of the votes in Congress on any issue
can be accurate without some understanding of the human
element of individual motivations of the members who
actually vote. Fortunately for the American system of representative government, many congressmen still do not
vote on the basis of polls or computed data. Most of the
Southerners who voted for multilateralist positions in
1953–62 accepted the fact that their votes would be a
political liability.

Mr. Lerche, however, suggested two far more accurate
descriptive labels, "unilateralist" and "multilateralist."
Lerche defines the unilateralist as one who leaves no room
for any community of American interests with the outside
world. The multilateralist, by contrast, believes that
American policy must be "built solidly upon a recognition
of the interdependence of all states [nations] for such
security and prosperity as they may enjoy." The Lerche
term for the unilateralist is especially fitting for the Southern members of Congress who have rejected all programs
with an international flavor, and for those constituents and

constituent pressure groups who have demanded this type of voting.

Why has such a large part of the Southern representation in the Congress turned its back on the long tradition of Southern internationalism? What has changed voting patterns, often in the face of what seems to be the obvious economic self-interest of the districts and states represented? As in all cases of governmental decisions, the answers are complex and not readily susceptible to identification by computer or any other form of political analysis which ignores the human equation in the decisions.

It has been common to ascribe the growth of Southern opposition to reciprocal trade and other internationalist programs to the growth of industry in the South, with the attendant demands for protection and the new ascendancy of the businessman over the farmer. This has not actually been the case, for much of the new protectionist vote has come from areas with a real economic interest in an expanded foreign trade. As an example, five out of six representatives from Mississippi voted the straight protectionist line on each of the last several occasions that the reciprocal trade program came before the House for a vote, even though the agricultural economy of the state was obviously one which benefited from liberal trade policies.

The growth of unilateralism has been part of a general deterioration in the quality of Southern political life as far as the Congress is concerned. The obvious cause is the increasingly dominant influence of racialism, grown more virulent in the past decade. The relationships between integration and the United Nations or between segregation and immigration policy may seem remote, but they have become very close in those parts of the South subject to the straitjacket of racist politics.

The United Nations has come to be regarded in much of the South as a tool of the new African states, manipulated by the Soviet Union. Most of the national political leaders who have been outspoken in their advocacy of the UN have also been outspoken in favor of civil rights. American civil rights efforts have been decried as mere efforts to gain the support of African and Asian countries. Immigration programs have been denounced as efforts to flood America with non-Anglo-Saxons and thus pave the way for more and more "vicious" civil rights programs and laws.

The leaders of organized resistance to school integration after the 1954 Supreme Court decision made a deliberate choice to align their followers with the right-wing extremist organizations and publications at the national level. The Mississippi Citizens Councils, for instance, circulated lists of publications like Gerald L. K. Smith's "The Cross and the Flag," Frank Britton's "American Nationalist," and Conde McGinley's "Common Sense," and a dozen others of the same stripe. Good segregationists were urged to subscribe, because these latter-day Know-Nothings were also opposed to integration. Very few additional citizens were converted to a segregationist philosophy by these tactics, but many politically unsophisticated Southerners were converted to a violent isolationism, quite often for no other reason than extremist support of segregation. They were also converted in large numbers to anti-Semitism, anti-Catholicism, and many other doctrines of the devil theory of government. This was a fertile planting of the seeds that bloomed into a major revival of the Ku Klux Klan and other terrorist organizations.

The failure of this alignment with the fringe elements of the Know-Nothing movement in the country has been made clear by recent political events. The forces of the radical extremists have been augmented by some Deep South political force; but, though the segregation movement itself has lost rather than gained ground, unilateralism as a power in congressional decisions has been given major impetus.

As our foreign aid program moved farther away from Europe and assistance primarily to white men, its popularity declined in the South. Congressional supporters of foreign aid have been assailed on the stump by the assertion that any step which leads to further American involvement in foreign affairs will inevitably speed the progress of integration. The more America is involved in the affairs of the world, so this theory goes, the more she will seek the approval of black, brown, and yellow men by ignoring racial distinctions. The moral is obvious—anything foreign has overtones of integration.

Some of these rabid assertions that anything international means liberalism, which automatically means integration, have been beaten back by skilled politicians, but many of them have been used with murderous effect. Dozens of members of Congress (and ex-members) carry their scars. The most important influence of racism on Southern Congressional attitudes has been a more indirect one, however. Racial politics have provided an easy path to election and reelection for the average national legislator from the Deep South; there has been far more political mileage in opposition to than in support of foreign policy. There has been no need to debate, on any intellectual level, any issue other than race. Subject to these influences, the quality of new membership deteriorated, and the qualities of those already in the Congress deteriorated from ill-use and timidity.

Racist influences also diminished the support at home from those limited groups which have, by tradition, contributed to the political support of congressmen taking internationalist positions. Most of the newspapers, professional people, and others of the intellectual community with normally the greatest interest in foreign affairs were either absorbed in, or more likely overwhelmed by, the racial tide. Their value as political assets was greatly diminished. The timid congressman dependent upon them had to give up early.

The most outspoken leaders of the unilateralist philosophy in the Congress largely have been Southerners, and some of them have become well-known national figures because of their activity. Being a villain in most of the national press has always been a political asset in the South, and the unilateralists have capitalized on every unfavorable mention in New York, Washington, London, or Moscow, often making very little distinction between the presses of the cities mentioned.

A few of the prominent unilateralists in the tradition of Cole Blease and Bob Reynolds are dedicated believers of their own doctrine, convinced that they have a burden to save the nation. Most of them, however, are simply politicians seeking the easiest route to reelection.

One of the healthy aspects of Jeffersonianism has been the resistance to granting arbitrary power to the President. Racism, however, has perverted Southern support of this sound doctrine into a concept of almost total opposition to all the powers of the presidency. The worst example of this in recent years was the strong support for the Bricker Amendment which developed among otherwise reasonably good constitutional lawyers in the Senate from the South. The Bricker Amendment would virtually have barred the President from making international agreements. It was rejected in the Senate, the one place it could have been stopped, by the narrowest of margins, and the few Southern votes preserved at that time are due eternal credit.

Some of the obvious weaknesses of our foreign aid program make votes on this annual authorization less than an ideal measure of a congressman's internationalist feelings. In basic practicality, however, there is no other real meas-

ure. When the Know-Nothings line up in total opposition,
the conscientious internationalist has had no other choice
than to support the bill finally brought to a vote, the
alternative being complete rejection of the entire concept
of American leadership in international cooperation.

During the past decade in the House of Representatives
the members with outspoken unilateralist philosophies
have voted solidly against all foreign aid bills. Another
large group has veered back and forth, depending upon the
extent of isolationist feeling in the district and the
member's own immediate political problems. Those who
have consistently voted for the foreign aid programs have
done so with the knowledge that they were voting in opposition to the prevailing popular sentiment in their districts,
and they have thus taken on an added political burden for
the time of their own reelection testing. Many of the more
politically vulnerable have stayed ahead of these hazards
by an educational effort among their constituents to explain the necessity for foreign aid votes. They have
accepted the responsibility that a member of Congress has
to inform his constituents of the problems of government,
rather than merely listen for the ripples of the gathering
storms of public opinion.

In a number of districts where racism has been the
dominant political issue, incumbents have been defeated
by opponents who made the members' support of foreign
aid a potent part of their platform. In most cases where
they have tried to inform their constituents about the issue

and their position, the members have been strong enough to avoid defeat. In other words, most of the members who met their responsibility of attempting to lead public opinion rather than to follow it have been successful in winning reelection in spite of the handicap of unpopular votes on international issues. Their comparative success points the way for similar action on the race issue.

The South has drifted away from its solid traditional support of the internationalist position because racism has become all-encompassing, touching every international issue, and because racist domination of politics has reduced the overall quality of congressional representation. It has limited the effectiveness, the energy, and the ambition of the most qualified Southerners in Congress, and it has largely eliminated the opportunity for full and free debate of foreign policy and international issues in the relatively limited Southern intellectual circles.

There are, of course, obvious and distinguished exceptions to these generalities about the mediocrity of Southern representation in Congress on foreign policy issues. Their distinctiveness is increased by their limited numbers, and their considerable ability for genuine achievement in this field is handicapped by their constituency.

The heartening signs that at least the major portion of the South is emerging from the political thralldom of the race issue offer great hope for a vigorous attack on the unilateralist foreign policy viewpoint that has become so dominant. In the past, Southern political leadership in

Congress has been uniquely qualified for leadership in foreign policy discussions both in the nation and in the South. We can hope that conditions are improving enough for Southerners again to have that opportunity and to have the will and the courage to take advantage of it.

The Pattern of Southern Congressional Politics

FOR MORE THAN A CENTURY THE INFLUENCE OF RACISM, and race-oriented issues, has been the dominant theme in the representation of the Deep South in the Congress of the United States. At times during the first forty years of this century the all-encompassing dominance of the issue seemed to recede, but it began to grow again with Negro emergence during World War II and became completely obsessive after the 1954 Supreme Court school desegregation decision.

Beyond race, the most predominant characteristic of Deep South politics has been the one-party system. Since the one-party system owes its existence to the race issue, it is perhaps not proper to distinguish this as a separate characteristic. For practical purposes, one-party politics has been confined to the state level for the last twenty years, and the race issue has long since shattered the once "Solid South." Many state political leaders are still primarily concerned with keeping race as the dominant issue in national political contests, and some of them are still wistfully hoping that the Republican party will maintain its white-supremacy stance so that they can tack their local structure, en masse, onto that of the Republicans. The local leaders would not turn over the party; they would still expect to stay in power.

State officials and other local politicians with no national responsibility have in the past few years become the chief incendiaries of Southern racism. They are, of course, the chief beneficiaries of a one-party system.

Perhaps the only positive value of the Goldwater presidential campaign in 1964 was the impetus it gave to the two-party system in the Deep South. (In many parts of the border and upper South, the Goldwater candidacy was as harmful to local Republicans as it was in the rest of the country.) The efforts of national Republican leaders to console themselves with the thought that they had created a two-party system in the Deep South should be taken with a heavy grain of salt, however. Before 1964 the great bulk of the Deep South Republican vote was in the cities and suburbs. In 1964 the big gains were largely concentrated in the small towns and rural areas. Most of the Southern voters who marked their ballot for a Republican for the first time regarded themselves as voting for the conservative candidate, but their definition of "conservative" was one who opposed the 1964 Civil Rights Act. When Mississippi voted 87 percent for the Republican electors (the white voters more than 90 percent), it was not a two-party development, but a massive shift from the know-nothing, no-party position to another party. The unanimity of the vote was little different from the one-party days prior to World War II.

The Republican vote in the Deep South may mean that a major portion of those voters and state politicians who regard preservation of segregation as the chief purpose of their ballot have at least turned their backs on the old concepts of "unpledged" electors and/or a Dixiecrat party. Attempts to sell this idea to the mass of voters broke down before the attractions of a candidate like Goldwater.

The immediate question to be decided in 1968 is whether the new allegiance to Republicanism will be strong enough to embrace a Republican candidate for President who endorses an active civil rights program and vigorously campaigns for Negro votes on the inevitable grounds that the Democrats have not achieved enough results. The 1968 Republican candidate will be drawn from a field of potentials who could be classified from almost any part of the conservative to liberal spectrum, but it is inconceivable that the nominee will be anyone who has not supported civil rights legislation.

With such a Republican candidate, another effort will be made in at least some of the Deep South states to form a third party ticket with the blessing of state and local office-holders. (The unpledged elector scheme might be put forward again, but there is a good chance that by 1968 it will be barred by constitutional amendment or some effective statutory method.) Too many conservatives in most of the Deep South states will prove too committed to Republicanism and too much involved in the fight for party control in the 1968 convention, however, to desert their new party. They will also be too disillusioned about the illusory goal of persuading the rest of the country about civil rights. This prediction may not hold true for Mississippi, still the least politically sophisticated of the states, because of the added factor of national Democratic party commitment to Negro participation in party affairs in all the states. Bitterness may still be strong enough in Mississippi to reject all association with Democrats, and it may carry over in opposition to a Republican "sell-out."

Undoubtedly, there will be a third-party ticket with considerable strength in the Deep South, for such a party will get national support from national far-rights who will talk of the same Republican "sell-out." The question will be whether or not this right-wing operation will be respectable enough to carry one of the Southern states.

The major influence of the Negro vote in the Southern states in 1964 has been commented on at length. It obviously will continue into 1968, but probably not with the same one-sided effect. The most important new development in this field will be the increased percentage of Negro registrants in the states where their voting is still resisted. Continued Negro pressure and massive federal efforts to enforce the various voting-rights laws will in some instances more or less break down local resistance as useless. Despite the impressive vote totals, only about one third of the potential Negro voters in the South were registered in 1964. A major breakthrough in the enforcement of federal law, or more effective laws, might result in twice that percentage by 1968.

According to a report made early in 1965 by the Southern Regional Council, 1,962,000 Negroes were registered to vote in the eleven Southern states. This is at least 750,000 more than were registered ten years earlier. The percentage of adult Negroes registered ranged from 69.4 percent in Tennessee to 6.7 in Mississippi.

In these eleven states, 12,300,000 votes were cast in the 1964 presidential election. Registration is no sure indication of voting participation, however; so it would be inaccurate to presume that nearly 2,000,000 of these were Negroes. The sharp increase in Negroes qualified to vote within the decade, however, will obviously be continued.

The rate of increase, by states, is shown as follows:

State	Qualified Negroes 1956	Qualified Negroes 1964	Percentage Now Qualified
Alabama	53,336	104,000	23%
Arkansas	69,677	105,000	49.3
Florida	148,703	240,616	63.7
Georgia	163,389	240,000	44
Louisiana	161,410	162,866	32
Mississippi	20,000	28,500	6.7
North Carolina	135,000	248,000	46.8
South Carolina	99,890	127,000	38.8
Tennessee	90,000	211,000	69.4
Texas	214,000	375,000	57.7
Virginia	82,603	121,000	45.7
Total	1,238,038	1,962,682	39.8

The Freedom party affair and the resulting action of the Democratic National Convention have made it impossible for the party to back away from its commitment to seat no future delegations which have not been chosen with Negro participation. Mississippi is the one state where this requirement could still conceivably result in a lily-white Republican party and a predominantly Negro Democratic party. The odds are still against such a result, even in the state which has taken the most extreme political positions.

The absence in future years of a sharp racial issue such as existed in 1964 will not only weaken one of the Republican sources of strength in the Deep South, but it will also weaken the tendency of the Negroes to vote solidly Democratic. Despite the pro-civil rights stance of future national Republican candidates, the congressional candidates of the Deep South Republican party are likely to be much stronger segregationists than the Democrats for the next few elections. No matter what the previous record of the Democrats, they will be aligned with a national party linked in the Southern mind with the Negro revolution, and this link will carry forward even if the civil rights issue fades faster than can be hopefully anticipated.

As the South moves toward that reality, a new breed of Southern politician is going to emerge. Southern politics, and congressional politics in particular, has been the prisoner of race for the past generation. In too many cases, the politicians were very willing prisoners. Some were not, of course, but too many welcomed the opportunity to pour gasoline on the flames, or to hitch the free ride. Since World War II it has taken little more than being "agin" to be a successful congressman from the Deep South. Successful means being reelected, which is, after all, the major measure of success in politics.

When the tragedy of our present racial strife is evaluated by some scholar in the distant future, two groups will be shown to have had the most reprehensible records: the demagogues who exploited the issue for political gain or as a cover to throw up legislative blockades to economic progress, and those in positions of responsibility who refused to use their powers of persuasion and leadership to bring acceptance of the Supreme Court decision of 1954.

Mississippi has the largest proportion of Negroes of any state, and since the Civil War it has always been on the lowest rung of the national economic ladder. These two not unrelated factors have not had directly equal influence on the politics of the state. Through the years, race has been a far greater influence than poverty. Where race is concerned in politics, the most extreme position has historically prevailed. Mississippi politics is accordingly a good index to the whole range of Southern political patterns.

From its admission to the Union in 1817 to its attempted secession in 1861, the state's economic and political leadership devoted itself to the creation of an agricultural economy and to the maintenance of slavery, the labor pool with which the economy became one of the most prosperous in the country. In the Reconstruction period between 1865 and 1890, that leadership reasserted itself, to reestablish the plantation system and ultimately to control its politics. The foundation was the same; only the semantics were different. Until 1865 the name was slavery; after 1865 the name was "white rule," or the Southern way of life, or states' rights, but the system was the same, whatever its label.

The corresponding historic dates for each of the Southern states are different, but the pattern, for all practical purposes, was identical to all. The economy of any region has a significant effect on its politics; this is not a characteristic peculiar to the South. (Neither, for that matter, is racism; the difference lies in the fact that in the South racism is simply more determined, more virulent, and more overt.) A population composed of a large number of almost totally uneducated Negroes, plus a sizable number of either uneducated or ill-educated whites, lent itself to the development of two forces. The first was a landowner-banker-business group, the Southern leadership, which materially benefited from a cheap labor force and thus had a real personal interest in maintaining the status quo, irrespective of moralities. The second was what has come to be known as the poor white group, a populace which included not only the small white farmer but the crafts and trades and service people as well. In the main unlettered and unskilled, this bulk of the white population was led to believe, by fact and by manipulated fear, that the freed Negro was his competitor and thereby his enemy. Turned upon the Negro by economic forces, excluded from the ruling society, the less solvent white rationalized a status for himself by assuming superiority to the Negro, or had it rationalized for him, and the creation of white supremacy was complete.

There is not a great deal of difference between the kind of propaganda that was used to justify the segregation laws enacted by Southern legislatures following Reconstruction and the kind of so-called states' rights doctrine spread by Governor Wallace early in 1964. Both were designed to persuade the white man that the Negro would ruin him financially. Given any degree of economic or social insecurity, this type of persuasion becomes very powerful. It was

powerful in the 1890's and is today; and whether the target
is a low-income Polish group in Milwaukee or the low-
income Anglo-Saxons in Maryland's money-pinched bay-
shore counties or the Deep South's even more money-
pinched rural areas makes little difference. The appeal is
the same, and it works. It works better in the Deep South
because for successive generations, white Southerners have
been assured of their superiority by the press, the bar, the
church, and the politicians, each to their own interest.

From this foundation, conformity has been the common
denominator in Southern congressional politics since the
Civil War. From post-Reconstruction 1890 to the Great
Depression of 1930, the issue rose and fell as the transitory
racists who reached national prominence rose and fell. Its
absolute influence was seldom absent from local and state
politics, but for long periods it was not the major factor for
senators and representatives.

Traditionally, it has been popular to picture the typical
Southern congressman as the willing tool of various reac-
tionary economic interests—big planters, big business,
courthouse political rings, etc. This has often been true,
but in most cases the controlling element simply has been
that the politician in a one-party system has to make some
attempt to please every interest that has an influence with
the electorate.

Through the years much of the racial agitation among
Southerners in the Congress has been a vehicle to cover
attacks on liberal economic legislation. Seventy-five years

ago the Southern Bourbons used the race issue to defeat the Populist movement; the Southern Democrat-GOP coalition of the past generation was nailed down with the GOP promise (and occasional delivery) of assistance against civil rights measures. The greatest strength of the race issue, however, was in its use to defeat or handcuff congressmen or would-be congressmen who were interested in supporting federal programs to invigorate the economy of the South.

The political influence of farm migration and industrialization in the South has varied. Urbanization has focused some attention on the need for federal legislative remedies for urban problems, but the wide-spread growth of medium-sized small towns has largely been a conservative influence. Villages are dying out, but small towns have generally grown in population, and most of them are strongholds of anti-federal philosophy. Unionization in the South has not kept pace with industrial growth, and many of the union workers who are organized, including large locals of the United Automobile Workers and the United Electrical Workers, have given vocal and effective support to blatant racist politicians.

The Southern states are the poorest in the country, and Southern states receive by far the greatest ratio of assistance from federal grant-in-aid and welfare programs. Despite this, the fiercest opposition to these programs in recent years has come from Southern congressmen. One reason is that the chief beneficiary, the Negro, has been

disenfranchised. Another is that many of the programs
have been made unpopular with even the impoverished
section of the white electorate by being described as primarily of benefit to the Negro or likely to promote integration.

One of the national tragedies resulting from this greater
tragedy of the politics of race has been the loss of a broad
federal aid-to-education program during the post-World
War II years. During the 1930's and 1940's the majority of
Southern congressmen were committed to federal aid to
education. If this same degree of support had held, the
program would have been enacted into law under President Truman, with a resulting better-trained and-
educated generation today. The education program has
been the victim of many political machinations through
the years, but the nation's greatest loss came when these
benefits were denied to the first classes of the expanding
postwar population.

This shift in sentiment on education was only one example. Beginning in the late 1930's, with minute but meas-
urable Negro progress in economic and political rights, the
iron grip of a political pattern designed to resist any change
in the racial status quo began to tighten over all the
South. It made its appearance first as opposition to some
of the New Deal economic measures and developed considerably during World War II as various administrative
concessions to Negroes were made by President Roosevelt

in the midst of the war effort. After President Truman's civil rights commission made its report in 1947, the racial issue became the dominant consideration in every Deep South state and in the great majority of the House districts from the old Confederate states.

Since 1947, there has been no leeway on the race issue for Southern members of Congress; they have been tied irrevocably to the views of those who sponsored and supported the Dixiecrat movement of 1948. The leadership of the Southern bloc in Congress has not been confined to the open Dixiecrats, of course, but because racial extremists established the Southern position on civil rights in the Congress, a rigid posture of opposition to any change in race relations in the South has been forced upon the members from the South. Members from border areas were not as completely under its domination, but they also felt its influence.

Most of the Southern members are personally opposed to civil rights legislation, in one degree or another, of course. A few are rabid racists; most would be middle-of-the-road or open moderates if they could. But as white racists organized in the South under the impetus of the 1954 school desegregation decision, it became politically impossible for any Southern member of Congress to be identified as a moderate. The troubles of those who refused to sign the so-called "Southern Manifesto" made this clear, and each new election emphasized the point further. Many of the men, moderate in conscience, retained their seats in contests, but only at the price of becoming racists in their campaigns.

Thus for twenty years the Southern legislator has had to accept the fact that both his constituents and his colleagues considered that his chief responsibility in the Congress was unceasing opposition to any advance in Negro civil rights through federal legislation. Occasionally Southern members privately raised the view that civil rights legislation with a gradualist approach, written with Southern cooperation toward the goal of acceptance and compliance by the white South, would help to end the divisive abrasions within the Democratic party, to say nothing of meeting the legislative responsibility of the Congress. The one open Southern effort in this direction was the constitutional amendment to repeal the poll tax, and it was turned down by civil rights proponents as a violation of their concept of legislative remedy. (The amendment was not passed until President Kennedy gave it his support in 1962.) Proposals for any other type of gradualist civil rights legislation met violent opposition from the controlling Southerners, however, and none were made, even privately, after 1950.

Civil rights legislation has always passed the House of Representatives without important amendment whenever it came to a vote. The strategy of the Southern leadership has been to prefer strong bills, thereby ensuring that Southerners in the Senate would prevent passage. For the proponents of civil rights legislation, the problem was primarily to draft bills that were not too strong for the sometimes-reluctant support of Republicans or northern Democrats, officially on the line for civil rights but privately not very aggressive about it. Working on this combination, the Southern senators were able to block any civil rights measures prior to 1957. When Lyndon Johnson promoted the strategy that changed the 1957 bill to a voting rights measure, the Southern senators did not resist to the point of cloture, realizing that the right to vote was the one issue on which enough northern and western senators would not help them. The same consideration prevailed in 1960. In the House Southern members were denied any practical voice in shaping the bills, but Southerners had an important role in the Senate, as is evidenced today by some of the difficulties encountered in trying to use the federal courts to implement Negro voter registration drives in the South.

The 1964 civil rights bill was a different story in the Senate, after going through the usual process in the House, where the bill was revised to gain the full support of Republican leaders. The Southern senators gambled that they could prevent cloture. If they had any doubts about their strategy, Governor Wallace's forays into the North completely boxed them in, giving their constituents illusions of success in the fight against the whole bill and virtually making it impossible for the senators to retreat anywhere along the line. One result of their intransigence was the adoption of some amendments that lessened the impact of the bill on the North without change in its severity for the South. The fabled legislative acumen of Southern congressmen has been consistently thwarted in the field of shaping civil rights legislation, largely because they are unable to undertake any compromise. The success in preventing legislation other than the 1957, 1960, and 1964 civil rights bills has probably been overrated, for the minority dedicated to complete opposition to civil rights has rarely been matched by a majority with any real dedication to the task of passing the legislation. The Kennedy-Johnson effort of 1963–64 was the first time the full resources of a national administration were thrown into the fight.

The 1964 Civil Rights Act probably marks the last time that major opposition to such legislation will be built entirely around Southerners. There will be no overnight change of attitudes, but the pressures for rigid conformity will be less and less. With voting restrictions against Negroes confined to fewer and fewer states, Southern senators from states with no restrictions are not going to be in a position to take up the burden for two or three Deep South states.

Undoubtedly, there will be moves in the next few years to simplify the procedures under which the federal government can intervene to establish and protect the voting rights of Negro citizens in the South.* Congressional resist-

* This was written several months before President Johnson submitted the new voting rights legislation to the Congress. The new legislation will simply hasten the changes suggested in this essay.

ance to such legislation will probably stem from the Southerners, but beyond that civil rights will not be a regional political issue. The resulting freedom from the straitjacket of politics dominated by race will bring about a vastly different pattern of Southern congressional representation as we move into the next decade. The changes may not be discernible from one Congress to the next, but they will be readily apparent over a broader span of time. The court decisions requiring equal sizes of congressional districts will have important effect, but the greatest changes in Southern politics will come from the combination of universal Negro voting and the court decisions requiring reapportionment of state legislatures.

Racial demagoguery will carry less of a political premium, and there will be continued acceleration of the growth of a two-party system. Democrats from the cities and the poorer small towns and rural areas are likely to resemble more and more their northern liberal counterparts. The Republicans who gain office are likely to be staunch conservatives who will inherit the philosophical support of those who have been taught that all federal power is evil.

For the South as a whole, racism as a political force has probably reached its peak and begun the long decline. It will be felt, however, in subsidiary issues like foreign affairs for years to come. Too many voters have developed their entire concept of these issues in the light of their alleged influence on Negroes in the South. Long after all

legal discrimination is ended, even in Mississippi, Southerners will look askance at a world subject to African
influences.

Despite these handicaps, Southern politics will be more
and more free in the years to come. There are challenges in
the next decade to produce great governors who can carry
forward state programs to eliminate educational and economic inequalities, with Negroes participating as full
partners in both the planning and realization of the programs. There are opportunities in this same period for
young men to build national careers in the Congress without the millstone of racism to preclude their full participation in national decisions. The obstacles may still be
formidable, but there is before the rising generation of
Southerners a challenge to greatness that has not been
equalled since the time of Jefferson.

The Changing South

"COTTON IS GOING WEST, CATTLE ARE COMING EAST, NE-
groes are going North, and Yankees are coming South." *
This popular quip is more fact than fantasy, and it briefly
describes a great many of the changes through which the
South is passing in these middle years of the twentieth
century.

Today California would be second only to Texas as a
cotton-producing state except for the artificial restraint of
acreage controls. New Mexico and Arizona are important
parts of the cotton belt. Cotton is still the major Southern
agricultural commodity, but it is no longer king. The shift

* This chapter is reprinted from *The Virginia Quarterly Review*, Spring,
1955.

of cotton production to the Western states has come at the
same time the old cotton-producing states have become
major cattle producers. Texas is symbolic of the shift. The
East Texas of the Old South is rapidly becoming cattle
country, displacing cotton as the keystone of its agricultural economy. At the same time the West Texas country,
once considered usable only as part of the western cattle
range, has become the largest cotton-producing area of the
state, thanks to irrigation and mechanized cultivation and
harvesting.

The shift from cotton to cattle is not exchange of one
one-crop economy for another, but it is symbolic of a
healthy diversification of Southern agriculture. There is
still much to be accomplished toward diversification, but
it has today become an accepted goal throughout the
South. Part of the diversification achievements can be attributed to the enforced limitations upon cotton plantings at
various periods during the operation of the government
price-support program. At some future date, hindsight may
show the elimination of the one-crop system to have been
one of the major accomplishments of the restricted production program.

"Negroes going North and Yankees coming South" is the
story of both economic and political change. When the
mechanical cotton picker first appeared on the scene, there
were fearful cries about the human misery that would
result from the displacement of agricultural labor in the

South. Actually, the cotton picker and the less dramatic tractor have barely been able to keep up with the shortage of labor caused by migration to Southern cities and other parts of the country. This migration reached its greatest peak during World War II, but has continued throughout the postwar years, with only brief setbacks during periods of economic recession.

Industrialization has come to the South largely from the North. Insufficient local capital and know-how had handicapped industrialization of the South, and a vast part of the industrial development which has come since World War II is expansion of industries already established in other parts of the country. Instead of merely opening branch plants, many of these industries are now shifting their chief production to the South.

"Yankees in the South" is also a symbol of political change. The Republican party gained successes in 1952 which are likely to be less tenuous than those of 1928, even though most Southern states are still many years away from two-party status. Republican success has its greatest air of permanence where there is substantial industrial development, where there are the largest concentrations of population from the North.

The South is changing, but change is not new to the region. The changes have been under way since the failure of the bloody struggle to resist the great economic and social revolution that became imminent immediately pre-

ceding the Civil War. All change throughout the ninety
years since the war has been met with stubborn resistance,
but the change has inexorably come.

For twenty-five years after the failure of its war for inde-
pendence the South struggled through a period of sometimes still-violent mutation, attempting to establish economic and political order out of the chaos which existed at
the conclusion of the war. Reconstruction for the native
whites was an effort to reestablish domination in political
and economic affairs. They succeeded in gaining political
control at home, with some semblance of the reestablish-
ment of the plantation economy. But the poverty-stricken
region lacked the capital or the credit to give sound foundation to its economy, and the result was a colonial status
which was often extended into unknowing political control, in both Washington and the state capitals. The ex-
cesses of the Reconstruction struggle have also left their
mark on the region as it has sought to adjust itself to each
new period of American history, down to the present.

Reconstruction established a political pattern for the
South, but it did not control the economic goals to be
sought by the new political order. The Southern agricultural economy was a fertile ground for the new idea that
political action could eliminate some of the abundant agricultural poverty. The Populist movement was an early
symbol of the protest, but the Populists as such rarely
gained power because of the fear that such division might

restore political power to the black man. The Democrats in the South largely defeated the Populists by absorbing them and their program. At the national level this absorption of Populism was reflected in the enthusiastic support which William Jennings Bryan received in the South, and in the same enthusiasm for Woodrow Wilson's new freedom, both at the polls and from Southerners in the Congress. At the state level, practically every state named governors dedicated to economic and social reform during the period. The educational program set in motion by North Carolina's Governor Aycock just after the turn of the century is perhaps the best known and the most successful.

By any standard the accomplishments of the period were very limited, but the chief reason was the basic poverty that had existed since the Civil War turned the economy of the region upside down.

World War I gave most of the South its first taste of the industrialization that some of its leading citizens had been preaching for many years in the fashion of Henry Grady. The taste was good, and for ten years after the war industrial development was the theme of Southern business and political life. New industries came at a greater rate than ever before, but the rate of industrial expansion was still not as great as that of the country as a whole during the same period.

Except for the dollar cotton boom of 1919 and 1920, Southern agriculture was not a partner in the prosperity of the 1920's. The agricultural depression was a forerunner of the Great Depression, which ground its heel into the South more deeply than any part of the country.

The New Deal brought for the first time an opportunity to solve, through federal intervention, some of the economic problems which federal intervention had helped create seventy years before. The South eagerly supported all facets of the New Deal which offered the spending of federal money in the South. Consciously or not, there was a realization that lack of money was the basic Southern problem. Conservative forces shied away from some of the Roosevelt reform program, but there was no opportunity for effective resistance until World War II had brought a new kind of prosperity to much of the South. WPA and PWA and similar programs brought a relatively higher standard of living to much of the South than had been enjoyed for generations.

The most important part of the New Deal as far as the South was concerned was the farm program. The price-support program for the first time offered both an increase in farm income and some assurance of stability. The related agricultural programs of rural electrification, soil conservation and resource development, and expanded opportunity for farm ownership were also popular. Southern agriculture is now wedded to these or similar programs for years to come. The Southern farmer accepts the fact that farm prices are made in Washington, and he keeps a sharp eye in that direction.

World War II had vastly more influence upon the South than the obvious effect of heavy wartime spending. The catalytic force of that experience on the country as a whole has been doubly felt in the economic, social, and political life of the South. It is the impetus behind the accelerated change in the South today. Much of the change is economic progress offering men higher standards of living and better ways of life. Much of it is cultural and social change, often uncomprehended and often unwanted and resisted. Most of the change is as inevitable as the turn of the pages of history; part of it is a result of the peculiarly vast depth of need in the South.

The industrial expansion in the United States necessary to meet the needs of World War II was enlarged upon by the military mobilization program of the Korean War, built upon a relatively unrestricted civilian prosperity. This proof of the capacity of the American economy has revolutionized most thinking about peaceful goals for the economy. Today a President can speak of an immediate goal of $500 billion annual income for the country and receive cheers instead of jeers from his fellow conservative Republicans.

The South has profited proportionately more than any other section from this economic expansion. During the fifteen-year period which began with the outbreak of World War II in 1939, business volume in the South increased by 500 percent, farm income by 300 percent, and manufacturing output by 500 percent. Perhaps the most satisfactory measure of progress was the increase in per capita income from $381 to $1,305.

Industrial and commercial expansion have come to the South primarily because of the generally increased capacity of the country as a whole. Other factors have contributed to out-sized expansion. Firms faced with the necessity of costly rehabilitation of plants and machinery have determined that it is better business to build new sites where there are better climate, lower taxes, and less likelihood of labor difficulties. Wage differentials have been the decisive factor with some marginal industries, and others have come South through the combination of promotion and incentives offered by state governments with fine disregard of "free enterprise" dogma. Tax exemptions and free or cheap plant use have been chief among the incentives. Low-cost power has been a major contribution, although, contrary to widespread notions, all but a small fraction of the new generating capacity in the area has been supplied by private utilities.

The greater part of the industrial growth in the South is built upon a solid foundation which should survive all but major dislocations in the economy of the country. There is considerable marginal industry that has already shown its nature in periods of recession during the past two years, but even those communities which have felt the blow of the shutdown factory have generally reflected that the period of employment and paychecks was better than the complete void in existence before any plant operated.

Other economic influences are likely to affect wage differentials as new industrial developments survive the experimental stage. Competition for labor and unionization will become more important factors that will eventually make wages responsive to industrial and national rather than regional influences. At the same time the Southern advantages of climate, comparatively more efficient plant and equipment, and labor supply will become a bigger part of the picture.

There is good reason to believe economic expansion of the South will continue at the same rate during the next fifteen years. This will mean that many of the country's industries will be centered in the region, especially those using chemical and agricultural commodities as raw materials. There may be even a dozen cities in the neighborhood of the million mark in population. Service industries will continue to mushroom in line with the improvement in the per capita income of the people.

Greater individual income is bringing a higher standard of living to the people of the South, through the normal operation of the demand and supply system. There is better living also because all levels of government are more active in helping to provide it. One concise example is the experience of Mississippi in the eight years since the Hill-Burton hospital construction program first went into effect. During that time, while the state's population was remaining static, the patient days of service rendered by general hospitals in the state increased by 65 percent. It is simply the result of hospital beds becoming available for the great mass of the people for the first time.

New development may see larger home ownership and control of expanding business. Because of lack of capital and know-how, both money and management have largely been imported. Some of the state governments which have entered freely into industrial promotion have begun to see the possibilities of state action to channel local capital into new business. There has been even more active participation of local capital on its own initiative simply because local money is present for the first time. At the management-operative level, higher educational standards all down the line are offering greater opportunities for competent personnel for Southern business and industry.

Thanks to the impetus of an economic expansion completely interwoven with both the economy and the culture of the United States as a whole, the South may be about to begin the most far-reaching change it has experienced since the War Between the States. The region may be entering completely the mainstream of American life after a century of movement among the eddies and shallows and drifting outside the turbulence.

In 1865 a young federal officer inspected a Mississippi plantation home and commented:

The literature of the family library was quite ancient. Dryden, Scott, Shakespeare, Pope, Swift, Byron, and Johnson were to be found there. Also Voltaire and Paine, Adams,

Madison and Jefferson were there; but Calhoun, Webster, Clay and Benton appeared to be favorites. . . . Of course, I looked in vain for a scrap from such advanced thinkers as Gerrit Smith, Garrison, Phillips, Sumner, Lowell or Whittier, or even Seward or Emerson.

Much of the criticism of the cultural backwardness of the South through the years has had more or less this same flavor, but even the most violent Southern partisans have to accept the fact that the region produced only Edgar Allan Poe as a major literary figure until well into the twentieth century. After Jefferson and Madison there were no national philosophers, though Calhoun deserves rank as a student and philosopher of government whose theories have profoundly influenced the destiny of our country.

The acid pen of H. L. Mencken was also dipped into the exaggeration traditional of critics of the South when he described the region as a cultural Sahara in 1920. Mr. Mencken was probably right when he said that "in all that Gargantuan paradise of the fourth-rate, there is not a single picture gallery worth going into, or a single orchestra capable of playing the nine symphonies of Beethoven, or a single opera house, or a single theater devoted to decent plays." He did not point out that all of these accoutrements of culture require ample financial support, and that money was not present and had not been for some time. Today, with money considerably more free, the void described has been filled. Even before prosperity and tax laws began to encourage the endowment of cultural enterprises in the

South, state and local governments were taking action in the field, by contrast with some less conservative parts of the country. A small but effective example is the state-endowed Barter Theater at Abingdon, Virginia.

In the field of higher education, Southern universities are not likely ever to reach a position comparable with the great endowed institutions like Harvard, Yale, Columbia, Princeton, and Chicago. There are limits in this field that might not be met by even the fabled Texas millionaires. Southern state universities, however, can be compared with almost any group of state schools over the country. When the limited resources available to support these schools are taken into consideration, the comparison usually can be favorable.

At the same time that Mr. Mencken complained, in 1920, of the lack of opera houses in the South, he said that except for James Branch Cabell ". . . you will not find a single Southern prose writer who can actually write. . . ." Glossing over the possibility of an argument about Cabell, even as Mencken was writing, Southerners such as William Faulkner, Thomas Wolfe, and Ellen Glasgow were writing or about to write the works that have made the statement ridiculous.

During this post-Mencken period, American literature has gone through a cycle of the Southern novel in a manner not far removed from the cycle of the proletarian novel and the Freudian novel. The most able Southern writers, however, are no longer classified as "Southern" writers. Each new artist may be compared with other Southern writers, but they are no longer discarded to a special limbo because of that fact. It will never be possible to evaluate a writer like Faulkner without an understanding of the distinctive Southern influences in which he lived and of which he wrote, but it is possible to consider him and others as creative artists, instead of as freaks escaped from the swampland.

There is some truth in the quip that book sales are so low in Mississippi (or substitute any other Southern state) because the people are so busy writing books they don't have time to read them. Actually, the sales record has been low because the income figure has also been low, and there has been less stress upon the educational and environmental influences which encourage book readers. The continued economic development and expansion is certain to bring changes in the cultural indices of book sales and magazine subscriptions. The creative artist in the South today finds as much encouragement as anywhere in the country, probably more than in most areas. Other than the still important fact that the South's economic level is yet below the national average, there are certainly no unfavorable factors.

Political changes which have come to the South during the past decade are sometimes more apparent than real. The one big change is the increasing respectability of the Republican party. This relatively favorable atmosphere for Republicans, as well as for some of those who maintain the Democratic label but oppose all national Democratic policy, is likely to continue as long as economic conditions remain generally prosperous. Although much of the Republican success in 1928 in carrying several Southern states for Herbert Hoover is today attributed to the religious and prohibition issues injected into the campaign, it is significant that the times were relatively prosperous. As mentioned earlier, appreciable opposition to Franklin Roosevelt and the New Deal did not make material headway in the South until wartime prosperity had eased some of the depression pangs.

In 1952 the personal popularity of President Eisenhower and the generally unfavorable reaction to the Democratic administration of President Truman were the major factors in Republican success in the South. This success also came during a period of general prosperity, but the chief cause of the dissatisfaction with President Truman was the civil rights program which the President and the national Democratic party had supported. Eisenhower supporters claimed a position satisfactory to the South on this issue. The Eisenhower administrative actions in the field of civil rights and racial matters generally have very likely neutralized or eliminated the civil rights issue from future Republican and Democratic conflict in the South. With Republicans no longer able to claim anti-civil rights records, they are unlikely to achieve any spectacular results for years to come. The 1956 election will show a decline in Republican presidential strength in the South, no matter who the party nominees. If economic conditions are not favorable in the election year, the Republican decline could be spectacular.

Bitter factional fights within the Democratic party will continue to be the rule instead of the exception in the Southern states. The causes will continue to vary from factionalisms and personalities to standard "liberal versus conservative." If the history of the first half of the twentieth century can be used as a guide, some of the political leaders who take the most extreme stands on racial issues will also be radical on economic matters. This will be in the tradition of Vardaman, Tom Watson, and Bilbo.

The South has gained an undeserved reputation over the years as a producer of demagogues and buffoons among its political leaders. Certainly the region has given prominence to a fair share of politicians who fit this description, but in no greater proportion than other parts of the country. Perhaps the reputation was built up because all other sections could self-righteously disclaim "bigotry," thanks to the absence of a racial factor in state politics. Recent developments indicate that this atmosphere may be changing.

Through the recent past Southern representation in Congress has made significant contributions to governmental policy which appear sound and farsighted from the present vantage point of hindsight. Although major New Deal economic reforms were enacted with overwhelming Southern support, it was Southern opposition which halted the Supreme Court packing plan. Perhaps other motivations than preservation of traditional safeguards for constitutional liberty entered into the historic court fight. The net effect, however, was to strengthen the tradition of the constitutional system. Southern influence in the more recent congressional controversies involving investigative power and abuses has been on the side of adequate safeguards to protect the individual rights of citizens and the proper division of powers within the government. Few Southerners have been in the forefront of agitation around these issues, but the eventual weight of Southern influence has been the deciding factor in each step toward the elimination of abuses.

At that critical period when it appeared that the United States was about to abandon the draft of soldiers just a few weeks before American entrance into World War II, it was a solid block of Southern votes which prevented the senseless and dangerous confusion that would have resulted. Southern congressmen were generally ahead of the field in awakening to the dangers of isolation prior to World War II, just as they had led the fight in trying to achieve Woodrow Wilson's goal of membership in the League of Nations. Today Southerners have the chief responsibility for the legislative defense of the policies of an internationally minded Republican President, at a time when his own party cannot furnish the leadership to implement his program through the Congress.

In recent years the South has felt a relatively sharp increase in isolationist sentiment, even though such thinking is still in the overall minority. In part this has been because of the growing influence of protectionist elements within the new industrial and agricultural development. The chief cause has probably been the influence of the minor national fetish of anti-intellectualism. The growing awareness in American business of the international responsibilities of our government, plus the continuing influence of a strong Southern tradition, should serve to checkmate this development before it gains a stronger hold.

On economic matters Southerners in the Congress today have a reputation for conservatism which does not always stand up under scrutiny. There is a strong resistance to planned programs or blueprints which bear any of the earmarks of the doctrinaire liberal or "New Dealer," but against this is an even stronger support for measures in the old Populist tradition of more money for the average man, or greater economic opportunity for the development of a resource or region. An important influence on thinking about labor legislation is the effect upon the various industrialization efforts. Voters with little money and still-restricted job opportunities will remain the decisive influence in Southern elections for years.

Defense of the institution of slavery was the one nongeographic common bond of the Confederate States of America. Today the one nongeographic bond held by all the South in common, aside from the bitter heritage of the

Confederacy, is acceptance of a system of segregation in basic social relationships between Negroes and whites. Segregation practices have differed through the years in various regions of the South, but the accepted and basic purpose has been to maintain a separate social relationship. Through the years since the Reconstruction period, vast progress was made toward establishing a peaceful and orderly relationship, built within the pattern of social segregation. Other artificial barriers fell away in the process by mutual consent. The best example of the progress being made is the fact that the Southern Negro's economic gains during the past few years have been proportionately even greater than those of the white man and that economic exploitation based on race has virtually ended. Another proud milestone has been the virtual disappearance of lynching as a symptom of racial discord and conflict, by contrast with a period at the beginning of the century when it was accepted and stoutly defended as part of the normal way of life.

Southern political leaders at the national level secured acceptance of their ousting of Reconstruction governments at the price of a series of informal agreements to accept national developments which began with the election contest of Rutherford B. Hayes. For twenty-five years thereafter they fought successfully against a series of "force bills" designed to restore federal control over state elections. During the next forty years there were sporadic talk and occasional gestures toward national legislation affecting racial relationships in the South, but no serious efforts were made along the line.

The vast human and economic mobilization of World War II gave new energy to the forces which believed that the American Negro's problems of relationship with his fellow citizens could be solved by legislative prescription. Repeated efforts to pass such laws made resistance to the so-called civil rights legislation the chief effort of Southern legislators in the Congress. Many forces entered the fight, on one side or the other, with no real concern about the outcome, but in the hope of achieving their own camouflaged goals. After "civil rights" had become a spectacular issue in the 1948 presidential campaign, the major attempt to pass legislation in the field was made in the fight to modify the United States Senate rules in order to eliminate the filibuster. When this attempt met defeat, political realists accepted the fact that no major civil rights legislation could pass the Senate in the foreseeable future. Any future federal action in the field would have to come through executive regulations or judicial edicts.

Administrative action in the civil rights field has become an accepted pattern. There is no likelihood that any future administration will fail to act to achieve such goals, after the demonstration of the effectiveness of executive regulation made by the Eisenhower administration.

The Supreme Court ruling against segregated schools struck at the heart of the effort to preserve a system of social segregation. It made a mere bugaboo of threatened fair-employment-practices legislation, previously regarded as the most fearful of the civil rights legislative plans. The ruling found only a tiny minority of Southern whites ready to accept it. Even among Negro leaders there is considerable confusion about an acceptable method of implementing the decision without bringing about educational setbacks for their children or stirring further racial discord.

All Southern states are in the process of resisting the implementation of the decision through the full power of state governments. At this writing the Supreme Court has not yet ruled in regard to implementation, so that the various steps toward resistance which have been taken in the South are still on a tentative basis. Once there is a ruling as to implementation, it is safe to assume that the strength of resistance to the decision and order will vary largely with the proportion of Negro population in the various states. Barring some type of provocation which would make federal enforcement of the ruling a strong issue in the rest of the country, a few Southern states, or at least sections of those where there is a predominant percentage of Negro population, will not accept the ruling at any time in the foreseeable future. Some parts of the South will accept some form of an integrated system only if the present migration pattern continues to sharply reduce the Negro population.

Racial attitudes in the South have changed over the years, but the changes have not involved any general acceptance of the type of society that the idea of a nonsegregated school invokes in the average Southerner. The fact that local hysteria failed to develop as an immediate reaction to the decision did not mean that attitudes were conditioned to acceptance of the new idea.

The great tragedy of the segregation decision has been the grave setback felt in the progress made toward good relations between the races. Mutual suspicion and distrust have become more prevalent again. Firebrand extremists on both sides of the issue have assumed positions of leadership instead of reasonable and rational men. Tensions have increased in some areas to the extent that they can be likened to the smoldering brush ready to erupt into a raging forest fire of violence if any strong wind comes along to fan the flames.

The problem is one that concerns not just the South, but the whole country. In a larger sense it invites concern from the whole world, for new sectional discord here could destroy the effectiveness of American world leadership. A century ago the nation approached a similar problem, and extremists prevailed in both North and South, with disastrous results from any viewpoint of the national welfare. The problem today is by no means completely identical, but there is sufficient similarity to make temperate leadership a vital necessity. Imprudent interference from outside at this particular period could cause grave consequences at the national level for years to come.

The Supreme Court decision, no matter how it is or is

not implemented, may eventually be recognized as a milestone in the final transition of a changing South. Economic developments are at last foretelling a period when the South and Southerners will have a completely equal share in the nation's wealth. The continuing concentration of mediums of communication and other institutions of education and entertainment which influence the national culture entirely above the regional level will be felt even more strongly in the South as economic growth enables and encourages the Southerner to become susceptible to these influences. Willingly or not, and knowingly or not, the South is finally entering the mainstream of American life.

After another generation it may become a major objective of students to discover and outline the traces of the Old South still discernible in our national life.

The Emerging South

WHEN SENATOR BARRY GOLDWATER BROUGHT HIS PRESI-
dential campaign to East Tennessee in September, 1964,
he spoke from the Knoxville-Maryville airport, in the solid
Republican county of Blount. It is Parson Brownlow's
home country; at a rural cemetery a few miles away a
headstone proclaims the death of a local patriot, "mur-
dered by Confederates."

When Senator Goldwater spoke, however, the Confederates were out in much greater force than one hundred years
before. A large Confederate flag dominated the platform,
and smaller Rebel pennants were waved throughout the
crowd. Here was a candidate who spoke of "states' rights,"

and people with Confederate flags know that "states' rights" means segregation. The year 1964 was the hallmark of a decade of Southern resistance to racial change, and it was appropriate that the victory be symbolized in the once solid Union country of East Tennessee. The same year that saw all the segregation barriers finally broken, at least in token fashion, roused the first real hope in the Southern bastions of resistance that the tide would actually change in their favor.

The first signs became evident when there was outspoken opposition to the Kennedy-Johnson civil rights law in other sections of the country besides the South. Governor George Wallace of Alabama made impressive showings in Democratic presidential primaries in Wisconsin, Indiana, and Maryland. Stirred by the scent of victory, the Mississippi legislature financed a national lobby against the bill. Racial violence flared in a dozen points in the North and reached the riot stage in Harlem. At the San Francisco convention all the South watched as the forces of Senator Goldwater, who had voted against the civil rights law, turned aside the disorganized elements which attempted vainly to moderate the Republican platform. After years of resistance, nurtured largely among Southern leaders in the hope that national public opinion would swing to support continued segregation in the South, it appeared that finally the people of the rest of the country shared some of the same racist fears and biases.

The final Goldwater campaign effort was a television

spectacular beamed over the old Confederacy from Columbia, South Carolina. Fabled movie stars from California came to join old-line Southern politicians being retreaded as Republicans. Across the old Dixiecrat belt the elixir worked. Georgia was added to Alabama, Mississippi, Louisiana, and South Carolina. Mississippians who had voted 90 percent for Strom Thurmond in 1948, now voted with him 87 percent as Goldwater Republicans. In its traditional insistence upon conformity, the state most committed to resistance had acquired near unanimity in its first vote since Reconstruction for a Republican presidential candidate.

Mississippi gave Goldwater a larger percentage of its vote than any of the 44 states carried by Johnson gave the President, but even majorities like this failed to give the Republicans the majority of the popular vote in the South as a whole. The electoral vote, of course, went two to one for Johnson.

The two most significant developments of the 1964 election in the South, viewed in relation to national politics and to the history of the region, were Goldwater's victory in the five states where racist political philosophy is strongest, and the virtually solid anti-Goldwater vote of the Negro throughout the Southern states. The 1964 Republican philosophy, as enunciated by both the candidate and the platform, attracted the Deep South, but it repelled so much of the rest of the country that the Republican party will undoubtedly make a fetish of returning to active support of civil rights and an assiduous courtship of Negro votes in 1968. The goal will be more than merely the recapture of the Negro vote; the party will be striving to shed the label that now proclaims it a Dixie-oriented and -dominated party.

Negro votes made the difference between Johnson and Goldwater in Virginia, Florida, Arkansas, Tennessee, and possibly North Carolina. They also supplied the winning margin in several House and Senate contests in these same states. For the first time, Democrats in these areas are fully realizing the advantage of such an asset, and the local Republicans who deliberately set their courses against soliciting Negro support now recognize the nature of the price they paid to prove themselves better segregationists than the Dixiecrats.

The one positive benefit of the 1964 campaign, to the South and to the nation, is the impetus gained in bringing a two-party system to the South. The gains are not as great as they appear on the surface, despite the uniqueness of Republican victories in Georgia, Alabama, and Mississippi, but they have wiped out forever any allegiance to the Democratic party based on the Civil War and Reconstruction. (The Civil War Republicanism of parts of the mountainous regions of Tennessee, Kentucky, Virginia, and North Carolina has proved to be considerably more hardy, surviving even a dose of temporary allegiance to FDR and the New Deal.) Effective two-party political systems for most of the South are still in the making, but revolutionary changes in Southern political life are obviously one of the major results of the long decade of bitter-end resistance to integration.

The entire 1954–64 decade was a struggle for emergence by those forces in the South which were willing to grant the Negro full citizenship, either from allegiance to the American ideal of liberty and justice, or because the detour to fight over the issue was recognized as a major roadblock to badly needed economic progress. The 1964 election was as close as possible to a specific referendum on the issue of Southern emergence, and it proved that all except the Deep South states were willing to move forward, even if only after a hard struggle.

The long-predicted two-party status is not going to develop automatically as a result of the Goldwater surge in states previously immune to Republican presidential candidates. National Republicans are not going to allow the image of a Southern-oriented and -dominated party to continue, and a good part of the Southern Republican vote will vanish when the party loses its identity as the local white man's party. The adjustments will continue through two or three more presidential elections; but the South as a whole has begun to respond to national issues, and it will, therefore, become less and less a separately contested area. What future regional emphasis there is will be more and more on economic issues.

Even so close to the event, it is apparent that this election will be the most significant political milestone in the story of the emerging South. For the South as a whole, emergence into the greater national identity will be far more rapid than in the past. The bitter-end Deep South opposition to racial change will still be a major drag on economic and social progress, but 1964 will be recognized even in Mississippi as the year that clearly translated the handwriting on the wall.

Civil rights has been the all-obsessive issue in the South since the time of the President's Civil Rights Commission report in 1947, but to most of the white South until 1954 it was a vague threat of something coming in the far distant future. The school desegregation decision was regarded as an immediately fearsome threat of all the horrors of integration. Where the general public was not aroused by spontaneous combustion, political leaders, armed with a more concrete threat to wave before the voters, stepped into the breach to whip up the frenzy. Any review of the South in the past decade must give priority to the complete dominance of the racial issue at every level, not only in politics, but in economic, religious, and social affairs.

The story of Southern resistance to school integration, which quickly broadened into massive resistance to any change in the established barriers of segregation, has been well reported, and many worthy scholars are in the process of analyzing it. The central theme, from the day of the long-anticipated decision of the Supreme Court, is the failure of those in positions of responsibility to meet the challenge to secure peaceable, rapid, and orderly compliance with the decision. With the advantage of hindsight it is easy to assess responsibility for this failure; but it is still important that the assessment be made, because assumption of responsibility is still lagging at the local level ten years later.

The worst failure was at the presidential level. Not until there was physical resistance in Little Rock three years after the decision did President Eisenhower take decisive action to support the law and the Court. There would have been no magic compliance with the court decision if the President had spoken up for it, but there would certainly have been far less bitterness in its acceptance; and the bewildered moderates in the South, seeking a leader to rally behind, would have had a ready-made one. A presidential position, even a modest and reluctant one, would have been enough for many legal, religious, and educational leaders to unite behind, and they might even have attracted some political figures. When historic evaluations are made in the still distant future, President Eisenhower's failure here will be a major blight on his record in the White House.

No other national figure was available to fill the vacuum left by Eisenhower's failure to provide the leadership the situation demanded. There was no comparable Democratic leader, and Democratic pronouncements on the issue were either muted or dismissed as partisan politics. The Supreme Court itself became an object of nonpartisan scorn and abuse, from both rabid segregationists and the

rapidly growing right wing extremists. The American Bar
Association signally failed to give any effective support to
the decision as the law of the land. All of the attacks on the
Hughes Court made in 1937 were dusted off by those who
sought a national position for their attacks on the Warren
Court, while the more crude and direct critics simply assailed the mental competence and even the loyalty of the
Justices. Whatever the attack, however, the mass of Southerners accepted each one as a defense of segregation.

Much well-deserved criticism has been lodged against
various categories of leaders in the South for their failure
to speak out against the evil and injustice of a segregated
society. Much of the criticism is entirely valid, but too
many who make it have not been well aware of the reasons
which restrained countless white Southerners from facing
up to the challenge of conscience with which they were
confronted. Politicians barred from office, preachers removed from their pulpits, lawyers denied their clients or
rendered completely ineffective before judge and jury,
businessmen stripped of the assets of a lifetime were exam-
ples that few men could ignore, even if they were prepared
to risk the social ostracism and allied pressures mobilized
by the more volatile segregationists.

The actual use of physical violence against both life and
property, or the well-substantiated threat of both, did not
develop for white people until late in the decade. It always
existed for Negroes, and there were, consequently, relatively few Negroes in the South who were ready to speak

out for full rights in the early days of this past decade of struggle. Only when they were shamed by the courageous dedication of the young men and women who began the sit-in movement did the great mass of Negroes in the South make a major commitment to the civil rights revolution. Negroes as well as whites debased the once honorable position of "moderate" on the issue, and most of them did it out of sheer necessity for survival.

Thanks to the void in national leadership, there was little opportunity for the average Southern leader in any field to take a position of outright opposition to segregation and racial injustice which he could hope to sustain. Failing this, there still should have been room for more overt support of a realistic moderate position. Cautious and conservative men at least should have been able to speak out against the wildfire growth of groups like the Citizens Councils, to say nothing of more rabid organizations (ranging through a dozen names, but in reality new and more ruthless revivals of the Ku Klux Klan). In too many otherwise normal Southern communities only the actual perpetration of Klan-type outrages could bring responsible local leaders to speak out, and then almost always with the justification that the outrages served to defeat the purpose of maintaining segregation or repelling the Northern invader.

In the South perhaps the chief indictment for failure to maintain a climate of moderation, or even one where discussion was possible, must be returned against the churches and the newspapers. If ever a moral issue existed on which churchmen could unite, defense of a moderate position for open discussion of the race issue and opposition to the new hate groups was that issue. Outspoken individual clergymen learned that as individuals few of them could successfully take such a position, but they could have taken it as united churchmen supported by the various hierarchies of their churches. Failure to unite in defense of the position has resulted in the careful picking off of those whose conscience would not allow them to keep silent, and thus made even more difficult the present essential reconciliation of the church with full Negro participation in the life of the community, religious and otherwise.

The church was not brave, with notable individual exceptions, but neither was another institution supposedly proud of a tradition of freedom. Southern newspapers as a whole (once again there were notable individual exceptions) failed to raise their editorial voices in defense of a moderate position, and, even worse, failed to present a full and accurate picture in their news columns of what was going on. Far too many of them sensationalized every development from a strident, segregationist viewpoint, and did little to tone down their defamatory presentation until the local business community began to point out the economic consequences of continued racial strife.

The newspaper in a directly competitive situation has some justification for avoiding the economic retaliation

that could completely destroy generations of family investment and achievement, even though such a prudent stand
is not very much in keeping with the tradition of the
fighting editor or freedom of the press. In most towns and
cities of the South, however, the economic facts of journal-
istic life had long since developed newspaper monopolies
which were largely invulnerable. This has been proven
by those papers that were willing to face the organized
wrath of the segregationist groups. Many have suffered,
but the only ones which failed were country weeklies vulnerable to the destructive competition that could be established with little investment by the organized opposition.

Some of the newspapers failed to meet the challenge
because their owners and editors were in full agreement
with the extreme segregationist position. Others stood
aside because of a growing tendency to avoid speaking out
on any controversial issue. Many deliberately stayed out of
the fight, or joined it on the side of the segregationists, even
though they fully realized the racist position was doomed
to failure, because they saw the whole resistance movement
as a medium for advancing a brand of economic and political conservatism that would otherwise have little appeal for
either their readers or their political leaders.

Whatever their calling, sympathetic Southerners
avoided positions of open moderation sometimes simply to
avoid being different and often to avoid economic or physical retaliation. In the midst of the Negro revolution, the

successful local leadership faced up to the problem by initiating positions of racial accommodation only with the complete and usually openly acknowledged backing of the local economic power structure. Late in 1964 the small city of McComb, Mississippi, was able to act only over the signed endorsement of more than 650 prominent local residents, joined together to avoid reprisals. Over the entire South there could have been the same strength of unity in local leadership far earlier if those traditionally responsible for leadership had been willing to assume that responsibility.

In the decade ahead the dominant economic theme for the Southern political economy is likely to be the one subdued since World War II by the racial issue—the widespread search for new industrial opportunity. Some doctrinaires still true to the new political conservatism are likely to say that industrial development can best be achieved by cessation of all economic activity by the federal government (except for more restrictive tariffs and import quotas), but they are almost certain to be ignored by Republicans, Democrats, Dixiecrats, and Goldwaterites alike. Full-scale activity in the development of new industry has long been accepted as a major role of state and local government in the South, and these programs will be emphasized even more in the years ahead as the South seeks economic equality with the rest of the nation.

Industry-hunting techniques have been refined far beyond the old system of tax concessions and local coopera-

tion to keep out the unions, though these will continue to
be used. Both state and local governments have learned to
utilize federal programs and grants for the various community facilities essential to attract industry, and even to plan
for them. For many years the Mississippi Agricultural and
Industrial Board used grants from the Housing and Home
Finance Agency to finance its planning functions, even
though federal housing ventures were virtually barred
from the state, and the Mississippians in Congress were
dutifully vigorous in their opposition to the entire concept
of federal activity in the housing field. Federal assistance in
community industrial development under the Area Rede-
velopment Administration programs, the Anti-Poverty
Program, Accelerated Public Works, and the forthcoming
Appalachian Development Agency will be utilized even
more fully. Bugaboos about segregation and the 1964 political atmosphere resulted in some of the states and counties which needed help the most being the slowest to take
advantage of the various forms of assistance. The situation
is almost certain to be remedied as soon as the results begin
to show up in the cooperating counties. Since there is some
likelihood that Congress will finance the program more
generously in the future, the failure of early participation
may not bring long-range penalties.

Most of the forms of state and local assistance to new and
expanding industries have already been explored in the
South. Tax concessions have been supplemented by capital, usually for real estate and buildings, but sometimes for

equipment and other essentials through local bond issues. Various new devices for both capital and operating subsidies will probably be tried, as industries shop among the states and communities for the best bargains for their not often venturesome capital. Because there is a limit to this kind of community investment, however, there will probably be more and more demand for federal assistance. There have already been some reasonably successful efforts to use federal job retraining programs to beat minimum and union wage scales.

Competition for industry is an all-American operation, not confined to Southern states. In the past few years most of the Southern states have learned that their labor reserves are less and less attractive because they lack the skills needed more and more for automated operations. Trade schools have begun to spring up throughout the South as part of state and local school systems. There still is no realistic awareness of a generally more important educational deficiency—poor preparation in basic reading and writing skills which leaves the worker unprepared to absorb either special instruction or daily on-the-job details. When this educational deficiency is translated into a handicap to industrial development, it will bring more demand for state educational efforts and far more support for the only obvious solution to the grave educational crisis—full-scale federal assistance at all levels instead of the present patchwork of federal aid, designed primarily with the view of what could be squeezed past the Congress.

Unemployment in the South as a whole is more or less along the national average, but *under*employment has long been the reservoir used for labor for new industrial expansion. Even this supply will grow very limited in the years immediately ahead, however. This will be a factor in tapping the greatest supply of underemployed labor—the Southern Negro. Various provisions of the Civil Rights Act, including voting, will be the other major influence.

The industrial-promotion efforts of the past have usually left the Negro out, except as a remote and indirect beneficiary. Federal law, local Negro political power, and the simple demands for even more manpower mean that he will not be left out in the future. The problem of utilizing Negro talent and labor should offer fewer difficulties than ever before.

In the South as a whole during this past decade of obsession with racial issues, both races have shared in economic progress. Some of the same factors which reduced old regional barriers and helped break down resistance to racial change also were involved in the economic changes. In the states where resistance to social change has been the greatest, however, Negroes have received a disproportionately small share of the economic improvement.

In Mississippi, for example, during the decade 1950–60, the median income for white families increased by 121 percent, from $1,614 to $3,565, while the median for non-whites increased by only 97 percent, from $601 to $1,168. The proportion of Negro population in the state decreased during this period, and at the same time the concentration of nonwhites in the lower income groups increased. Of all families in Mississippi with incomes under $3,000, 49.5 percent in 1950 were nonwhite, and by 1960, 53 percent of this group was nonwhite. There is no evidence to indicate that the trend has not continued during the five years since the 1960 census.

The reasons for this comparative decline in Negro income in Mississippi can be found apparently in the pattern of migration out of the state. Migrants have been young people not fully identified in the work force as well as families with the highest incomes and obviously better training than those left behind. This type of migration has been normal for both whites and Negroes in the past. The changed figures indicate that an even larger proportion of the most productive Negro citizens has chosen to leave and that economic reprisals taken against upper-income Negroes have been sufficient to affect the total income pattern for nonwhites in the state. Industrialization programs which ignore Negro labor may also be part of the reason.

The areas of large Negro population in the Deep South would be identified as more serious "pockets of poverty" than Appalachia if a racial breakdown could be made in the statistics. Awareness of this, plus a realization of the long-range impact the loss of the most talented and industrious Negro students will have, should influence economic developments in the decade ahead. Scientific and technical

training is woefully inadequate in the Negro colleges of the
South, but those students who specialize in these subjects
almost always leave the South to seek employment for their
special skills. In the integrated colleges of the years ahead
there may be some realization of the goal of retaining this
talent in the South, both for its immediate individual
value and for the example that will be set for the use of
Negro manpower in expanding industrial development.

The destruction of the Southern economy in the Civil
War subjected the region to a kind of economic colonialism that has been widely acknowledged as equivalent to
that which existed in some parts of the British Empire in
the 19th century. Political colonialism obviously existed
also, but the present emergence is obviously in the process
of throwing it off. Is the economic colonialism also being
abolished?

Actually, it was the beginning of the emergence from
economic colonialism which brought the first stirrings of
the Negro revolution in the South. In 1933 the region
could best be compared with the status today of some of
the Latin American countries which are classified as un-
derdeveloped. The federal programs begun under the New
Deal, some directed especially at the South and some of
which merely received special emphasis in the South, still
rank as the best modern example of how a government can
develop a backward economy. There was an infusion of
money which alleviated some of the immediate suffering,
but the long-range investment was in land reform. Land

reform is not as radical as it sounds. It consisted of soil conservation, flood control, reforestation, price supports, farm credit agencies, public buildings and roads, schools, and river development. Other types of government credit provided a basis for local capital to meet local needs.

The Southern economy is still behind the national average, but the most severe handicaps in the economic field were eased by federal government action a generation ago. The major remaining hardship is the failure to utilize the supply of Negro manpower properly. A combination of the Negro revolution and pressure for manpower by the local economic developers is in the process of eliminating this hardship. Economic colonialism will be gone. The American economic system puts control of capital largely in the hands of banks which operate in the main centers of population, but this will be the accident of a centralized economy in the future, no longer one of the economic results (as well as motivations) of the Civil War.

If we are finally seeing the emerging South, it is only because the elimination of racial barriers was essential to the final elimination of both political and economic colonialism. In the mainstream of American life, much of the Southern identity will be lost, but if "Southern identity" is the price to be paid for removal of the racial scar which has been the mark of things Southern, both the South and the country will have gained thereby.

Political and economic changes will mean that the South

is emerging, not into one of the many often-heralded "New Souths" but into full participation in American life, with less and less regional identity. This will inevitably be accompanied by changes in the regional cultural patterns. For a long time the changes are likely to be more real than apparent.

Since the first all-pervading awareness of the South as a separate identity began to develop a century and a quarter ago, Southerners of every philosophical bent have attempted to give every part of their life and society a regional coloration. The racial bigots, the moderates, and the liberals have followed this pattern. So have both the illiterate and the highly literate. The burden of conscience that has been the heritage of every creative mind in the South for generations has been responsible largely for the special regional concept of Southern writers. There is certain to be a new literature of the Negro revolution, but once that is past what reason for special regional identity will exist?

In the South, without a special burden of responsibility for the Negro, there will be no reason for a literature built around either defense or apology. Too much of the insistence on the distinctiveness of the South and Southerners is in actuality only the defensive pattern that has been a regional characteristic since it first became necessary to mobilize in defense of slavery. Too much of the problem of the region and its people has been the refusal to accept a national heritage and to give allegiance to national ideals. The only reason for this, of course, has been the mobilized defense of the racial status quo.

There are distinctive regional influences among Americans, and there is an honorable heritage of Southern distinctions. So much of the heritage has been subverted into the defense of racialism, however, that the "Southern" image is tarnished, not only in national eyes but almost irretrievably among Southern Negroes.

It is possible that the emerging South eventually will be identifiable only as a geographic region that is the southeastern part of the United States, an area that was historically significant as composed of the states which attempted to form the Confederate States of America. Perhaps the goal for the Southern regional enthusiasts of the future should be to identify and preserve those characteristics that were not developed as part of a regional defense of a racial pattern foreign to the central American theme of freedom and justice.

Perhaps the years immediately ahead, more than any others of this century, will make clear the South's emergence. Surely every conceivable barrier to this emergence has now been breached.